LIFE DOESN'T **JUST** GO ON...

A Memoir

By Shanea Abriel Strachan

Life Doesn't JUST Go On
by Shanea Abriel Strachan

Signalman Publishing
www.signalmanpublishing.com
email: info@signalmanpublishing.com
Kissimmee, Florida

ISBN: 978-1-935991-64-9

Typeset in Adobe Garamond Pro
Interior Design by Joel Ramnaraine

SIGNALMAN
PUBLISHING

Dedicated to everyone who has recently lost someone or has ever lost someone and is experiencing grief.

Life Doesn't JUST Go On...

In Loving Memory of my Dad
Edwin Frederick Strachan II
July 25th, 1961 – December 27th, 2010

TABLE OF CONTENTS

ACKNOWLEDGMENTS

I would first like to give thanks to my Lord and Savior, Jesus Christ. I have been blessed to have so many amazing people in my life.

To my mom, Glenda, words cannot express how much I love you. You have been my biggest supporter and my #1 fan from day one. You have raised me to be the strong, intelligent young woman that I am today. Your love, your guidance and your struggle have molded and shaped me to be a caring, loving, giving and appreciative person. I know and understand your struggles and I am grateful for all of the sacrifices that you have made and continue to make for Shanique and myself. I once told you that I see my first million by 25, well I see your retirement by 50! My success is your success and I promise that I will continue to make you proud.

My little sister Shanique, thank you for your artwork in my book. I am happy that you are a part of this and that I can share your talent with the world. You are a very talented and smart young girl and I encourage you to stay focused on what is important right now and that is school. I am blessed to have you as my sister and I love you very much.

Grammy Golden, thank you for always being there to support me in one way or the other. I love you!

My big sister, Krissy, thank you for allowing me to use your poem in my book. Our relationship has come a long way, but I am thankful for where it's at and where it's going. Love you sis!

Julie, my friend and mentor, you met me when I was just 17 years old and you, more than any person, have seen the growth in me, spiritually and personally. Thank you for being an amazing friend, for always having your doors open and for helping me when I need it most. Thank you for your time, your friendship, your investment and your prayers. You will forever hold a spot in my heart.

Amy and Terry, two very incredible women. Two women who both know and understand the unfortunate pain of losing someone close. Thank you both for supporting me during the most difficult time in my life.

Terry, my coach and friend; thank you for always being there for me and for loving me unconditionally.

Amy, thank you for always having your doors open and for being so helpful and understanding.

I thank you both for your encouragement, support and motivation on seeing my book to completion.

To Colleen, thank you for your contributing words in my book, for all of your prayers and for helping me through everything.

To Stephanie, thank you for supporting me during my most difficult semester of college and even the semester after that. Thank you for always having your doors open and for always being there when I need you.

Mrs. Rojas, thank you for being a supporter. In my 21 years of life I can honestly say that you are the greatest teacher that I've ever known. It's been years since I've been in High School, but I want to thank you for everything you've done for me then and thank you for still being a part of my life now.

Last but not least, I would like to acknowledge my three best friends, Amanda, Evan and Leo. My Fab-4 friends, Chantelle, Karyn, Kara and Kahlil. Other family members including my brothers, sister, grandmother Lula, grandaunt

Yvonne, aunts, uncles, cousins and supporters back in the Bahamas. My friends and family in Florida, friends and supporters in Nebraska, Georgia and New Mexico. Thank you all for making an impact in my life. May this book be a blessing to you!

SPECIAL THANKS

I would like to dedicate this page to everyone who supported my IndieGogo fundraising campaign for the publication of this book.

To my friend, Maya, thank you for assisting me with the video production for my campaign page. Thank you for your creative insights, patience and support. I appreciate you very much.

Christiane 'Chrissy', you supported my campaign from day one! Thank you for your motivation, endless support and for being such an amazing friend.

Kahlil, thank you for your support and friendship. I am privileged to have you in my life.

Amy, I would like to thank you once again for your continued support.

Ron & Ellen, thank you both for your support and encouragement.

Eric, Dale & Valerie, thank you three for your friendship and your continued support and encouragement.

Tiffany 'T_low', thank you for being a wonderful friend. Thank you for your advice and for all of your support.

Aunt Yvonne, thank you for your support and encouragement in helping me see my book to completion.

I would also like to thank Niku Shaeri, Jacob Hadra, Kristoffer Kans and Wiebke Bruns. Because of the support from all of you, I am able to share my story with the world!

FOREWORD

Many of us have heard the expression "When life gives you lemons, make lemonade!" Shanea Strachan tells about the way in which she has taken this expression to heart. Her fascinating story begins in her home in the Bahamas, growing up in the challenging but all-too-common experience of a single-parent family. She takes the reader through the ups and downs of her life in a refreshing, honest way. She reveals the warmth of relationships with family and friends as well as the coldness of knowing there were family members she had never met. She opens her heart about the longing she experienced for a father who was present in her life when he was absent and the joys of the times when she did connect with him. She shares the rawness of her anger toward him as well as how she resolved her anger and reached out to him in a letter he never received. She walks you through the process of her grief after he passed away and how she dealt with it. Her story gives the reader a glimpse of how to respond to grief in one's own life as well as in the life of someone you care about. She demonstrates that it is never too late to connect with family members who were not previously a part of your life and the doors that open once anger and bitterness are laid aside.

Shanea combines poetry and narrative in a way that draws the reader in and connects you with her heart. I hope you are inspired, challenged, and instructed by this very personal and enlightening life story.

Dr. Colleen Stortvedt
Oasis Counseling Intl.

INTRODUCTION

Letter #1

Dear Daddy,

I hope everything is well with you. I wanted to send you a thank you card for coming through for me once again. I greatly appreciate it. I thought it would be cool to write you because I haven't spoken to you or seen you in years. I don't know, I feel kind of down today and I thought about you. Daddy people around me are dying and it really makes you think how precious life is. I lost my step-cousin two weeks ago; he was Alex's friend also. Alex was actually one of the Paul Bearers and my mom got a chance to speak with him. He has a beautiful son; I've seen his pictures on Facebook. I think you should get a Facebook :), so you can keep up to date with us. I am happy to say that I have Sasha, Alex, Estelle and Anthony on my Facebook. Daddy I wish we were a lot closer, but it seems like everyone is just caught up in their own lives. I want so badly to know my family and to have a strong relationship with everyone, but daddy I'm just tired of reaching out. It really makes me sad the way things are. It seems that death is the only thing that brings a family together and it shouldn't have to be that way.

But in all honesty I really want to feel like I belong. I use to think when I was younger that maybe if I was famous then maybe I could have my family because I do really want those relationships, even with you. Daddy you know I was at a place where I was so bitter and angry at you and I spent two months in Counseling just talking about you because I always felt unloved and unwanted and I became such an angry person, but two months later I'm at a place where I have peace. I had to find it in myself to forgive and let go. I'm a born again Christian and I think the hardest struggle I faced was forgiveness. I knew I reached to that place when I told my therapist that I wouldn't have any angry words for you if I spoke to you again and I don't. I just pray to God to keep you safe and well.

I don't know how you're doing but I really hope all is well with you. I don't know why but in a sense I feel like I'm losing you and I don't want to lose you, which is weird because I never even had you. I miss you daddy, I miss having a dad and I feel sad because I think that it's going to be something that I never have. I guess I'm feeling this way because my Speech Coach leaves for Arizona to visit with her dad because he's in his last stages of Cancer. I don't want that to be me. You know daddy, I'm a very independent person with a lot of stubbornness and pride and I always think that I don't need help from people. That I don't need people in general because they're always going to let you down. But you know I realize that sometimes we just think that we have the answers to everything and that we're okay and there's nothing wrong with us. I was that same way and it really gets you in a dark place, but you know once you have people there to help you get through its amazing.

You know this summer I decided to go see a therapist because I realized that I was so angry, hurt and bitter about everything in my life and it was one of the best decisions I made in life. I am a new and different person because of it and trust me I have A LOT of pride. My mom doesn't even know. But I realize that if you need help then you should get it. People have this stigma that people who see a therapist are crazy. It's like if you had a pain in your body you would see a doctor. Emotional and psychological pains are that way, people hurt so they need to see someone to make those feelings go away. I guess what I'm saying is take care of yourself and just keep yourself well. If you need help physically or psychologically don't be afraid to get it. Life is precious and it's short so just live it to the best of you. I really do love you daddy. Take care, be safe and know that you are always in my thoughts and prayers.

Love Always,

Your Baby girl Shanea

In January of 2011 after arriving back to my apartment in Norfolk, Nebraska, I found this letter in one of my notebooks. This is a letter that I wrote to my dad in November of 2010. As a child growing up, I never really had a relationship with my dad. He was an alcoholic and he was an absent figure in my life and because of that I experienced many struggles and heartaches. Over the course of my life, I developed hate, bitterness and resentment towards my dad because of his absence. I became such a broken person from that. Within the year of 2010, things with my dad slowly changed. He started making attempts and was active in my life. His attempts made me forget about the past and focused more on repairing our broken relationship.

On December 27th, 2010 while at home in the Bahamas for the Christmas break, I received a phone call from my Aunt saying that my dad passed away. That phone call was the most devastating call that I ever received. My dad's death was very sudden and it hurt me deeply because I had just spoken with him several days before.

I remember going back to Norfolk, Nebraska, from the Bahamas, two weeks into the spring semester of my sophomore year of college to resume school, just two days after my father's funeral. Before settling in at home, I had dinner with a very good friend of mine who said to me the words that gave me one of the inspirations to write this book. It had been twenty-one days since the death of my dad and I found myself expressing my feelings of sadness to her. Her words back to me were, "Shay, it's been almost a month, come on you just can't be sad, life goes on..." I snapped back at her, angry at that statement. A statement that I have heard from people usually after the death of a loved one or usually after something tragic happens in a person's life.

I'd like to say that Life Doesn't **JUST** Go On... especially when you lose someone close to you or you lose someone that you have unfinished business with. I know this because I've experienced it and I'm living it. The death of my dad has opened my eyes to so many things and has changed me as a person for the better. After finding the letter that I wrote to him, something inside of me told that I needed to write this book. I am not a professional writer by any means, I'm just a young woman with a passion to share my story and a hope to change lives through doing that. Be encouraged as I take you on this journey that was and is my life.

CHAPTER ONE

THE STORY OF A MAN

You dropped your seed in the soil of life
9 months later then I came
That's what you did, just drop your seed
Took time to plant me but hesitated to give me your name
It's a shame, for the greatness I will become
Took two to make me but recognition will only be given to one
And that's my mom,
Who has fought hard to raise me for all of these years
Worked two jobs, shed many tears
School fees came and many days I got sick, bills went behind
and things got turned off quick
When things got hard and I couldn't do the things that I
wanted to do
My only question was, "Dad where are you?"
I don't understand
Why don't you just take the responsibility and be a man?
Now I'm here, afraid to love, afraid to trust,
to be in a relationship
Telling myself that I need to let go and be brave
But how could I love someone....
Without that love never given
The love that you should have gave!
But I refuse to let your absence hold me down
I refuse to hurt over this and I refuse to frown
I'm 17 years old now and I won't have it anymore
I've thrown away that key and I've locked that door.
And like I've said once and time again before
This time I'm through with you and with you I don't want
anything to do with you anymore!

MR. SPERM DONOR

A while back, I was at a friend's house and we were watching my playlist on YouTube. What came up on the playlist was a poetic tribute titled "Letter #6 – 1 Year Later..." that I wrote and recorded for the one year anniversary of my dad's death. I explained to my friend that it was about my dad's passing. The words came up,

"I can't tell you how much I miss you, or what I would give to just hug you or to kiss you." As the tribute continued a minute or so until the end, my friend's response to the lyrics surprised me.

"Ah! How can you miss someone so much if you were never that close to them?" she asked.

In that moment I was hurt by her response, but now writing this, it really got me thinking. How can we miss something that we never really had or for better words how can we miss someone that we never really knew? But I had a dad and even though he wasn't present in my life I missed him.

I sat for a while thinking about what would be the best way to better tell my story and immediately this poem came to my mind. I wrote Mr. Sperm Donor, when I was seventeen years old. A poem in which I feel would be the perfect introduction. For you to understand the entire story, we must first go back to the beginning.

The story of my relationship with my dad is one that I am sure that many people can relate to. My dad was an alcoholic and after years of alcohol abuse, his drinking unfortunately cost him his life. He was born in Nassau, Bahamas in July of 1961; he was the second of eight children. As a child growing up, my dad had a very difficult childhood, being raised in a physically abusive household. Despite his challenges at home, he had great dreams that he would fulfill. Before my dad turned 30, he was a successful police officer and pilot.

This was during the 80s and early 90s.

I came along in September of 1991; I was the last of his five children. I have four other siblings before me. A brother that was born in 1982, a sister that was born in 1983, another sister that came along in 1988 and a brother that was born in 1989. My oldest sister and my two brothers all share the same mother and my second oldest sister and I have different mothers. There was a lot of drama going on in those days as you can imagine between our mom's and my dad. He was "the ladies man" and he had everything going for him. The looks, the clothes, the money and the women. Back in the day, my dad was on top of his game, but he wouldn't stay at the top very long. I don't know when my dad's downfall came or what caused it, but he eventually ended up losing his job and everything he had.

My mom left my dad a year after I was born. I hadn't seen much of him during the first three years of my life. It wasn't until I was about six years old, when my dad came back into the picture. My dad and my mom never got back together, but he made attempts to be a part of my life. I remember one day when I was about six years old and my mom dropping me off at my Aunt Janet's house to spend the day with my dad. Aunt Janet was one of my dad's sister, the two of them were always very close. That day, he was so happy to see his baby girl. That's what my dad would call me. Baby Girl. I remember him being so loving and me sitting in his arms as he showed me cards and love letters that he had from when he and my mom were together. He told me that he still loved her. That day I remember very well. My oldest sister Estelle and my cousin Lyn was there and we played games like "Twee- Lee-lee" and "Slide- Push-Clap" outside in the yard and all the other games that young children play. It was a wonderful day.

The next time I remember spending time with my dad

had to be about a year or two later. This time it wasn't so wonderful. It was a Saturday afternoon. My mom was out grocery shopping and my cousin Dominique, my neighbor Chelsea and I was at home. We were outside playing in the yard when my dad pulled up into the driveway with a friend. Excited as always to see him, I ran up to his car to be greeted by a big hug and a kiss. My dad invited me to come with him, Chelsea and Dominique came along. He took me to Baskin-Robbins for ice cream and to the candy store. Then it was off to meet his girlfriend Diane. The ride to her house would be a very unpleasant one. As my dad drove, he and his friend were drinking alcohol. I can remember my dad pouring alcohol into their cups as the car swerved back and forth onto the road. Dominique, Chelsea and I sat in the backseat in fear, while the two continued drinking their alcohol and laughing aloud.

"Shanea, please tell them to take us home, we're going to get in trouble," Chelsea said with worry.

At the time, a part of me wanted to tell my dad to take us home but a part of me didn't. Despite my dad's drinking, I still loved him. Being a young child, I didn't understand what an alcoholic was. When my dad drank, he didn't treat me any differently than when he didn't, at least from what I can remember. We drove for some time until we finally arrived at Diane's house. She was an older lady, but she was very nice.

"Boy, Eddie, this child looks just like you and she have them same baby teeth you have," said Diane.

My dad and I both smiled. We didn't stay at Diane's house very long. After a short visit, my dad made his way to take us back to my house. As we got onto the main road, Dominique noticed that my mom's car was behind us. In the passenger's seat was Chelsea's mom and they didn't look very happy. My mom followed us all the way back to the house. I gave my dad a hug and a kiss and went inside. I don't remember what happened next, but I didn't see my dad for a long time after that.

On several occasions after that incident, my dad made surprise visits to our house, which my mom did not like. She would always ask him to leave. One day my dad showed up at our house and sent my older brother Alex to the door. I was sitting in the hallway listening when he asked my mom if I was home. My mom told him no and asked him to leave. That must have enraged him because the next thing I remember was my dad banging on the door, ringing the doorbell and demanding my mom to let him see me, while cursing at her. He stayed there for a while until the police came, forcing him to leave.

After that, I did see my dad very often. He had my number and he would call me from time to time. But I hardly ever saw him. At this point he was becoming an absent figure in my life. He started to make promises that he didn't keep. I remember one in particular, it was in October. Every year in the settlement of McLean's Town, was the "Annual Conch Cracking Festival". This was a festival that people looked forward to every year. "Conch Cracking" was an all-day affair that my mom took us to every year. I spoke to my dad the day before Conch Cracking and he told me that he was going to pick me up that day, to spend the day with him. I refused to go to the Festival with my mom because I wanted to spend the day with my dad. My mom left early that morning with my baby sister, while I stayed home and waited for my dad. I sat in the living room waiting for my dad. I got up to the sound of every car that passed by, I didn't go to the bathroom or even get anything to eat because I didn't want to miss him. Eventually morning turned into afternoon, afternoon turned into evening and evening turned into night, no dad in sight. I remember feeling so hurt about the situation. Hurt at the fact that my dad told me that he was going to come and pick me up and he never came. My dad was always inconsistent. Sometimes he would come through for me, other times he wouldn't. When I was in the 6th grade, my school sold t-shirts for 'One Bahamas Day'. I was one of the few students in my class in school uniform because I didn't have a t-shirt. At the time it wasn't in my mom's budget to purchase me a t-shirt so I decided to call my dad and see if he would bring me the money to purchase a shirt. He said yes. During lunch break I went to the office to see if I could call my dad again since I hadn't heard from him. When I got there, the office's secretary had a t-shirt waiting for me. She told me that my dad came in and paid for the shirt for me. I was so happy that he kept his promise.

That happy streak with my dad didn't last very long. The next time I reached out to my dad was around the time of my Sixth Grade Graduation. My mom did her very best with raising my little sister Sade and I and she did it all on her own. Sade, who was seven years younger than I, both attended a small private Christian School. Graduation came with a lot of different expenses. My dad did make contributions towards some of the expenses for my graduation, which I was grateful for, but the disappointment came when I invited him to my graduation ceremony and he was a no show.

My 6th grade graduation was a very big occasion in my life that I wanted my dad to a part of. I gave him the invitation in advance and he told me that he would be there and I believed that he would. I mean what dad would miss their daughter's 6th grade graduation? During the entire ceremony I sat up on stage looking out into the crowd hoping that I would see him sitting there in the audience and once again no dad in sight. At the end of the ceremony, I still looked around for my dad hoping that he was sitting somewhere and I missed him, but he wasn't there. I was so upset that I didn't want to celebrate. I told my mom that I was tired and just wanted to go home.

The next day with so much anger and hurt inside of me, I wrote my dad a letter. A letter telling him how much I hated him and how I didn't want anything to do with him anymore. I told him that I was cutting him off and if he ever tried to reach me or come by the house to see me that I would call the police for him. I really didn't mean some of the things that I wrote in that letter. After I sent the letter, I didn't see or hear from my dad for a really long time.

Once while I was at Wendy's sitting in the car waiting for my mom, my dad happened to be there. I wasn't excited to see him; neither did I give him a hug or a kiss. In fact, I didn't say anything to him. He came over to the car and said, "Baby this how you going to treat your daddy? You don't have to say anything to me but I want you to know that daddy love you."

That was the last time that I saw him in Freeport. My dad moved to Nassau, Bahamas and I didn't see or hear from him until many years later.

CHAPTER TWO
FAMILY BUSINESS PART I

Many days I sit and frown
Questioning myself, why weren't you ever around
Why within myself so many insecurities?
Why do I have to be the one to fight?
Why my relationship with my brothers, sisters and your family
isn't right.
See this is my pain.
Deep in my heart, so I'm letting it bleed
So these feelings can depart...
And I'm always here, questioning why?
Why weren't you ever around?
Why don't you care?
Why don't you make a change?
This is my pain.
You don't know how much I hurt,
Hurt to the point where I feel lower than dirt.
Hurt to the point where my emotions over take, to the point
where I felt like my conception was a mistake
You don't know how much my heartaches...
But this is my heartbreak, daddy this is my pain...
When will you make a change?

MY PAIN

I wrote *My Pain*, towards the end of the year in 2006. I was then 15 years old and focused on another area in my life which was Family Business. I was interested in finding out about the other half of me which was my dad's side of my family. I made contact with my dad and spoke to him, so I was somewhat at peace even though not much had changed. But now it wasn't my dad that I was focusing on, it was my older sisters. I've always had a longing for big sisters. My mom and my aunts were very close and I grew up seeing the positive relationships between sisters. The desire for big sisters came most when I was a teenager. I wanted big sisters like the ones that I watched on TV. Sisters that I could go to for advice or talk to about sex and all of the things that a teenager didn't feel comfortable talking to their parents about. I felt like my big sisters were exactly what I needed at this time in my life.

I knew of my two big sisters from my mom, but I never met them. I had seen my second oldest sister Sasha once in Wendy's while eating lunch. In fact, she and her mom were sitting at the table directly behind us. My oldest sister Estelle worked at my mom's job for a short period of time and I spoke to her once over the phone. My mom told me that Estelle was working at a local company which was located Downtown. I passed the building where she worked countless times until one day I finally decided to go in and see her. I remember the first day that I met Estelle. It was the last day of school. My best friend Alannah and I were downtown having lunch. We somehow passed the building where Estelle worked and I stopped and said to Alannah, "My sister works there."

"Well go in and see her," suggested Alannah.

I felt a deep pain in my stomach. I was very nervous. I'd never formally met Estelle and it wasn't like she was expecting me. I went inside and walked up to the glass window and asked if I could see Estelle.

"Who may I ask wants to see her?" the lady behind the glass asked smartly.

"Tell her this is Shanea," I responded.

"Estelle says she doesn't know a Shanea," she replied.

I was upset by her response. I thought that my sister didn't want to see me.

"Tell her that this is her sister, Shanea, and I only came to see who she was," I said, storming out of the building on the brink of tears.

I was half way pass the building when I heard a voice from behind calling my name. It was my sister. She came to apologize because she didn't realize it was me. She gave me her number and told me to text her sometime. I took her number and left. Meeting Estelle for the first time wasn't quite what I had imagined or expected. All in all, I was happy that we met and I had a number where I could contact her.

It wasn't until a week later before I decided to text Estelle. There were so many things that I wanted to ask her. I wanted to know everything! This was a very exciting time in my life to finally be communicating with one of my big sisters. That very same week, I got an invitation from Estelle to hang out. I accepted. It was an evening or so later when Estelle came by my house to pick me up. I don't know why but I was very nervous. It was so funny that every time my sister would ask me a question I would respond with, "Yes ma'am" or "No ma'am". She of course asked me not to do that [laughs], but it was just my way of being polite and respecting someone older. Estelle was 8 years older than I was so me being 15, I saw her has an adult even though she was my sister. That night we saw a movie, grabbed something to eat and did a lot of talking. I learned a lot about my dad's side of the family. At the end of the night my sister gave me the new Danity Kane CD then took me home. I enjoyed my night out with Estelle.

It was a week later when I saw Estelle again. She called me on a Saturday afternoon. Estelle and my other sister Sasha were together and she wanted me to meet her. A short while after the call they came by and picked me up. Estelle took Sasha and me to the beach. Sasha was home from college on Christmas break. She wasn't as warm as Estelle and she really didn't have much to say. Estelle did most of the talking. The three of us hanged out for about an hour before Estelle made her way back to my house. After leaving my sisters, I felt happy to have such cool sisters. I got both their email addresses and added them on my Instant Messenger. I tried my best to stay in contact with them. Sasha never really bothered much, but I communicated a lot with Estelle. We had a lot in common and we were both writers. My relationship with my sisters didn't take off like I thought it would. We were all just at different places in our lives. I prayed that God would bring us closer. I wanted to feel like I could call them a few times a week or get together with them every now and again, the same way my mom did with my aunts. I knew that with Sasha it would have been difficult because she was away in college, but I still hoped for the chance of getting to know her. Nothing much ever became of it. I spoke to Estelle every now and then and to Sasha once in a blue moon. At the time I felt like I was the only one trying to make things work. I asked God,

"What was the purpose of meeting my sisters if we weren't going to have a close relationship?"

I prayed a lot about it and while waiting for God to answer my prayers, I waited for holidays, birthdays and special occasions to find reasons to talk to them.

It was until summer of the next year that there was an answer to my prayers. I received a summer job with the Government Program working at the Police Station which was located Downtown. Sasha received employment with the Government Program as well and she was placed nearby at the Courthouse, which was also located Downtown. She worked with a friend a mine and we now had a mutual connection. I began chatting with her again, mostly short conversations.

I worked at the Police Station for two months. It wasn't until towards the end of the program that I finally got to see Sasha. Her 19th Birthday was coming up and I asked her if I could take her out for lunch for her birthday. She had said yes. I was happy that I was able to spend some time with Sasha. The day of her birthday, Sasha, my best friend Alannah, our mutual friend Dion and I, all met up for lunch. The four of us made the short walk to a restaurant. During our walk we talked about our dad briefly, she asked me when was that last time I heard from him, I told her I didn't know. We didn't talk about him for very long. We finally arrived at the restaurant. I ordered lunch for the both of us while she secured a table. Sasha saved me a seat next to her. The four of us ate lunch together and it was great. It was nice to celebrate with my sister for her birthday. At the end of lunch we all walked back Downtown and parted our separate ways back to our jobs. I really thought that lunch with Sasha would bring some sort of closeness with our relationship but it didn't, things still remained the same. At the end of the summer Sasha returned back to the states for school and I didn't hear from her often.

A few weeks later I met with Estelle for lunch. We met at a deli Downtown. It was nice to finally meet up with Estelle again. I hadn't seen her in months. There was a lot for us to catch up on. I was so happy to be spending time with my big sister until she told me that she was moving to the United States towards the end of the year. I was devastated. There went all of my hopes of ever having a close relationship with my big sisters. Sasha was already gone and now Estelle was leaving. I knew that even though Estelle and I communicated, our relationship would die if she moved to the States. If we hardly ever spoke to each other and we lived on the same island, what would change if we were in different countries? I was very sad at the end of lunch, but I respected and supported my sister's decision to move. I made attempts to see Estelle as much as I could before she left, but a lot of those attempts failed. After that I decided to leave things alone.

While things died down with my sisters, things started to pick up with my dad. It was now October and I was preparing to travel to Nassau for a class trip. I was happy that I could see my dad and finally get the chance to talk to him. My best friend Alannah and I were two of five students chosen out of my class, to travel to Nassau and research information on disabilities for a national exam. The five of us along with our two religious studies teachers, left for the four day trip to Nassau. When I arrived to Nassau, I immediately contact my Aunt Janet. We stayed at the Sheraton Resort on the Cable Beach Strip in Nassau. It was so ironic that my dad at the time was working on a construction job by that very same strip, just two hotels down from us.

I called my dad when I was settled. He said that he would try and see me before I went back to Freeport. It wasn't until my third day in Nassau that I finally got to see him. We were free for the day to just enjoy ourselves and I made plans to see my dad. Early that morning Alannah and I walked over to where my dad was working. I called him to let him know that I was on site and he came down right away. After 5 long years I finally saw my dad. That moment will be one that I will never forget. When my dad saw me, he gave me a big hug and a kiss. He was very happy to see me, just as I was happy to see him. In that moment, I forgot about all the questions that I waited for years to ask him. The past really didn't matter to me. My dad was very affectionate and through his affection I saw his love. He kissed me over and over again on my cheek and told me how beautiful I was. My dad asked me my plans for the evening and I told him that I was free. We made arrangements to spend time together. He gave me a hug and a kiss, told me that he loved me and that he would see me later.

Alannah and I went back to the hotel and enjoyed the rest of our day. I got permission from my mom and my teachers to spend the evening with my dad. We met around four in the evening when he got off from work. My dad and I got on a bus and started our journey. I was so happy to be with him and he was so happy to be with me. We talked about so many things during our bus ride. I told him about how I met Sasha and Estelle; we talked about my mom and about me. He did most of the talking. He talked about how big I'd gotten and how much I'd grown. Over and over during our ride, he apologized.

"Baby, I'm sorry that I wasn't there for you," he repeated.

"The past doesn't matter, you're here now," I replied.

My dad wasn't the best father, but there was no denying that he didn't love me or my siblings. His affection and his words of affirmation showed that. I remember a very special moment during our bus ride. My dad placed his hands on my face and told me that had eye's like my mom and everything from the eyes down was all him. He once again kissed me on the cheek and told me that I was bodaciously beautiful. That was the first time that I'd ever hear that word. His words and affection really meant a lot to me. For the first time in my life, I felt loved by my dad and I enjoyed being in his presence.

While all of this was great, I could tell that psychological-ly something wasn't right with my dad from the directions that our conversations went. I had a strong feeling that his drinking contributed to that. That day my dad trusted me with a secret that he kept, that I feel contributed to one of the reasons why he drank. I felt happy that my dad trusted me. In that moment I became more understanding towards him and his drinking. My dad wasn't drinking because he wanted to drink; he was drinking to cope with what he was dealing with on the inside. It didn't make it right that he was using alcohol as a coping method but it made some sort of sense to me. We finally came to the end of our bus ride and continued our journey on foot.

My dad walked briskly leading the way and I walked a short distance behind him. I felt proud walking with my dad. He walked with a bop and I walked with that very same bop. My mom always told me that I walked just like my dad. Before arriving to my dad's house, we stopped at a bar. I drank a bottle of Smirnoff, while my dad took a cou-ple shots of Tequila. After our drinks we continued on our journey and finally arrived at his house. When we got there I met my grandmother Mabel and my great-grandmother, who we called 'Mama'. This was the first time meeting my Mama. I talked to Grammy Mabel while my dad got settled. My dad came back into the room and asked me if I could lose out the micro braids in his hair. My dad fell asleep as I continued taking out his braids. I noticed that it was getting late and I had no idea of how I was going to get back to the hotel. I mentioned to Grammy Mabel that my teachers were taking us to Atlantis that night and I did want to miss it. Grammy Mabel woke my dad up and told him that I had to leave. He awoke in anger, enraged that Grammy Mabel was telling me that I had to leave. He took it the wrong way. My dad and my grandmother got into a very loud and heated argument. I'd never seen two people argue that way. Grammy Mabel demanded my dad to leave, he refused. Mama advised him to do the same, but he did not leave. Grammy Mabel went into the kitchen and returned with a hot kettle of water threatening to throw it on my dad if he didn't leave. At that moment I left the house. I stood outside the door in tears for a moment trying catch myself. I was so confused; I didn't know what to do or where to go. I didn't want to go back inside so I walked out to the streets.

I felt so afraid. I was on the streets of Nassau, lost with nowhere to go. I walked tracing my steps of the way that my dad and I came, which brought me out of the neighborhood and took me on to a main street. Finally after walking for a while I ran into a bus stop where a bus was loading, immediately I got on to the bus. I texted Alannah and told her to have our teacher call me. My teacher called right away.

"Shanea where are you?" asked my teacher.

"I'm on a bus," I replied.

"A bus!?!" she shouted with concern.

"Yes, a bus heading to the hotel," I said.

My teacher instructed me to get off the bus once we made a stop Downtown and I did just that. When I arrived Downtown I went to the nearest store and called my mom. In tears I began telling my mom everything that happened. She told me that everything was going to be okay and to just stay put until my teacher came.

About 15 minutes later my teacher arrived. I didn't have much to say and they could tell that something was wrong. It was hard for what had happened not to affect me. I felt so sad and it showed. We went to Fish Fry on Arawak Cay for dinner that evening. I didn't feel like being around my teachers or my other classmates, so I asked Alannah if she would come with me to the restroom. I shared with Alannah what happened. She told me not to worry about it. But how could I not worry about it? I kept thinking about my dad. I wanted to talk to him. I stepped away to the side for a second to call him and apologize for leaving. When I called he was upset. Upset over the fact that I just left and he felt disrespected. He said that he was angry at me for doing that. Hearing those words from him brought tears to my eyes. Angry at his words, I cursed at my dad and hanged up the phone. I wiped the tears from my eyes and found Alannah and headed back to the restaurant. After dinner that night, we went to the Atlantis Resort. Being at Atlantis brought me back into good spirits. Just seeing the beauty of the resort and all of the Marine life was very therapeutic for me.

The next evening around 6, we made our way to the airport. Before leaving Nassau, I called my dad to apologize to him for disrespecting the night before. He seemed very out of it and he didn't say much.

"I wanted to apologize to you for last night," I said.

"Okay baby," he replied.

"Well... it was nice seeing you, take care," I concluded.

"You too," he responded.

That was our conversation. I felt that it was right for me to apologize to my dad. I just didn't want to leave on bad terms with him. I left Nassau with the peace inside of me knowing that I apologized to my dad, but I left not knowing that this visit would be the last time I would spend with him or see him alive.

CHAPTER THREE
A WHOLE OTHER WORLD

Almost six years ago we started on this journey
Hard to believe it's coming to an end.
Six years of laughter, good times and bad
Memories that made us happy,
Some even sad.
Grade 7, it came like nothing and grade 7 it went so fast
Over-sized school bags and immature actions are now almost distant
memories of the past.
I can remember grade 8,
Now that's a year I will never forget
Me back in grade 8, I was the rudest thing ever yet.
Going to class late, tie always unsnapped, breaking all the rules,
Getting 9 demerits for chewing gum, back then I was a fool.
Grade 9 and grade 10 came; I really didn't bother much
Same old as always... classes, assignments, teachers, books and such.
Grade 11 if I could I would do it all over again.
Ducking classes and clowning around really catches up to you in the
end.
Grade 12 is now here, determined to make this year the best
Striving for only A's and B's making this year better than the rest.
Cherishing every moment because these days will quickly fly
Soon you know it graduation will be here and it will be time to say
goodbye.

HIGH SCHOOL

Whenever I meet people and I tell them that I'm from the Bahamas, there response would always be something like,

"The Bahamas!?!"

"Well what are you doing here?"

"Why would you want to leave the Bahamas?"

"Why would anyone want to leave paradise?"

What seemed like paradise to others didn't feel like paradise to me. I always wanted to live in the United States. "America... the land of opportunity." My dream was to move to California and become a famous actress, although as time went by that dream changed. My dreams were bigger than my little island and I knew that to achieve those dreams I needed to be in the States. I graduated high school at the age of 16 in June of 2008. After graduation I began working full-time at a resort as a switchboard operator. I was thankful to have a job right out of high school. I didn't know what my plans were going to be after graduation, but I had hopes of studying in the United States. Every day when I got home from work, I would spend time looking at colleges. Mostly in Florida because it was close to home. Prices of colleges in Florida were expensive and they were more than I knew my mom could afford. I searched for scholarships, but there wasn't much offered because my grades weren't that great and I wasn't very active in high school. My mom suggested that I start my first two years of college at the College of the Bahamas, which meant I would live at home, work and go to school. I didn't want to do that. I wanted to study abroad and pursue my dreams.

In the 10th grade during career assessments, I made the decision that I wanted to be a filmmaker. I wanted to write and produce movies that dealt with real life issues that could make a difference in the lives of others. I began screenwriting in the 11th grade and that year I wrote, directed and produced my first short film on a camcorder. I knew for a fact that filmmaking was what I wanted to do. I began searching for film schools and they were even more expensive than the schools in Florida. I spoke with my mom continuously about studying abroad and finding a school. I wanted to leave in January of the following year. I knew that with my mom's financial situation I would have to start small which meant a community college. I narrowed my search down to cheapest community colleges in the United States. Results showed up mostly in the Midwest, more so in Kansas and Nebraska. I didn't know anything much about those states, but I requested information on several schools.

A few weeks later college brochures came in the mail. I took interest in a small community college located in Norfolk, Nebraska. It was their 2-year Broadcasting: Radio & Television program that captured my interest. They offered an Associates of Applied Science in Broadcasting, which meant that in two years, I would be ready to work in a radio station or television station. This was my school! I finalized my plans and discussed them with my mom. She liked the college that I selected and gave me the okay to apply to the school. My mom let me knew off the back that she didn't have any money to send me in August but if I worked and saved my money we would see about January.

I did just that. I worked and saved up my money. I wanted to show my mom that I was serious about college. Together, she and I opened up a bank account and every week I deposited my paycheck into my bank account. I appreciated my mom for supporting my decisions. I knew that with her finances there were concerns of whether or not she could afford to send me abroad to school, but she still encouraged me to apply and save. My mom and I had faith that I would go abroad to school and we prayed to God that He would provide a way. One day God showed us that He heard our prayers.

Working as a switchboard operator, my main duties were to answer all the incoming calls for the resort and transfer them to different extensions. I would sit in my office for 7 hours every day answering the phone and transferring the calls. My job as a switchboard operator also required me to deal with a lot of the guests that stayed at the resort. One week at work, I became acquainted with one of the guests over the phone. He went by the name of Apostle Jones. I would mostly transfer his outgoing calls and take his house-keeping and maintenance reports, he was grateful for the work that I did for him. One day Apostle Jones stopped by my office to introduce himself and to thank me for doing such a great job.

Shortly after 5 one evening, my mom and I were making our way to the car and we crossed paths with Apostle Jones.

"Shanea and Shanea's mom, come over here," he said.

"The Holy Spirit spoke to me when you guys walked by and I wanted to speak with you."

"Mom, you've been under attack and I want you to know that no weapon formed against you shall prosper. Continue to pray and God will reveal it to you," he said.

At that time some wicked person had been doing what seemed to be obeah work around our house. We didn't know who was doing it and this was something that a lot of people didn't know about, but Apostle Jones who had never met my mom was able to prophesize that. The prophecy continued. Apostle Jones began to speak over my life.

"Shanea, I see you trying to do something with going away to school. I know that things are hard but I want you to have faith. God will make way," was his words.

That was the first time that I had ever experienced an encounter with prophecy. I believed everything that he told us that day.

My mom and I left speechless. That encounter with Apostle Jones confirmed that God heard our prayers. I didn't waste any time after that. I began my application process and sent in all my documents to the school. Within 2-3 weeks later I received my letter of acceptance, my I-20 and my housing information in the mail. I could see God working by how quickly and smoothly things were progressing. The next step after receiving my I-20 was to make an appointment with the U.S. Embassy in Nassau to apply for my Student Visa. My mom and I were able to schedule an appointment during the second week of December. I began communicating with my Aunt Janet again. I arrived in Nassau on the 14th of December and from the airport I went straight to the U.S. Embassy.

It was a very long and nerve wrecking process applying for my visa. I spent the entire day at the embassy waiting in line to see the immigration officer. After an hour, I made it to the first window where I submitted my first set of paperwork, two hours later I made it to the second window where I paid the fee for my visa application. The easy part was over. I waited patiently for several more hours for my interview with the immigration officer. As time went by I watched as people got interviewed. Some people were granted visas while others were denied. I was very nervous about my interview, I thought about how much money I would have wasted if I wasn't granted my visa. My time had finally come and I walked up to the window with faith. The immigration officer greeted me,

"Where are you going to school for your education?" she

asked.

"Norfolk, Nebraska," I replied.

"Who's paying for your education?" she asked.

"My mom and my aunt," I responded.

"Okay, you've been approved for your visa, come back tomorrow to pick it up."

I couldn't believe it. I took the receipt from the immigration officer and left the Embassy. When I got out I quietly screamed in excitement. I said a prayer and thanked God, then ran to a nearby restaurant to call my mom. I wanted to surprise her so I called her at work. My mom answered the phone,

"Mommy," I said with a sad voice.

"What happen, Shanea?" she asked with concern.

"I got my visa!" I screamed with excitement.

"And they only asked me two questions!"

My mom and I were both very happy and thankful. My Aunt Janet arrived shortly after that. That night I stayed with my Aunt Sidra. She was my dad's youngest sister. It was the first time meeting her. The next afternoon my Aunt Janet took me back to the Embassy to pick up my visa. I was granted my student visa for 5 years. I didn't see my dad during that visit to Nassau but I did spoke to him over the phone. I went back to Freeport that very same day.

My last month in Freeport was spent working and spending time with family and friends. I was scheduled to leave for school the first week in January. My family, friends and even some of my co-workers showed so much support with me leaving to study abroad. I was very thankful for their blessings. On the 9th of January, 2009, my mom, my little sister

Sade, my Aunt Susanne left Freeport to begin our journey to Nebraska. We drove from Fort Lauderdale, Florida all the way to Norfolk, Nebraska. It was a 27 hour drive. Nebraska was unlike anything that I had ever seen or experienced before. The weather was extremely cold and there were mountains of snow everywhere. When we arrived we checked into a hotel and rested for the night.

The next morning my mom, my little sister and I went to the college. I checked into the dorms and then we ate breakfast together before they left. I said my goodbyes to my mom; my sister and my aunt and they were off. I was sad when they left but I was also very happy to finally be in college and on my own. It took a while for me to adjust to Norfolk. It was a very big culture shock and I was very homesick. I didn't talk to my mom or my friends often because I didn't have a computer and the ones at the college were blocked. Emailing was my only way of communicating with family and friends back home. I became involved in a Christian Student Fellowship group where I made some new friends. About two and a half weeks into the semester, I came across a flyer in the hallway. The flyer was for the Speech & Debate Team, which was recruiting new members. The flyer also noted that scholarships were available. Immediately I went in and spoke with the Coach of the Speech Team. She asked me about my experience in Speech & Debate. I mentioned to her that I debated in High School. That day I signed the scholarship application for a Partial Scholarship and became a member of the Speech & Debate Team. I received a Half-Tuition Waiver Scholarship and was refunded back half of my college tuition.

I was thankful, for yet another blessing from God. I couldn't wait to call my mom! She was very proud. When I received the refund check in the mail, I sent it back home to my mom. She deserved it. It was because of her support that

I was studying abroad in college. I competed on the Speech & Debate Team for my first semester of college on a Partial Scholarship and then went on a Full Scholarship after that. Apostle Jones' prophesy was true. God did make a way and for my first two and half years of college, my tuition was covered.

CHAPTER FOUR

AND THEN I TURNED 18...

How do you reach the light?
When you see the light as being so far out
And all of your thoughts of getting well
Soon become thoughts of doubt
When you've gotten to the point, where you don't even want to try
Because the pain has gotten so deep, that it hurts just to cry
When all you have left to live for is to die
And you soon come to know that everything you've been told is a lie
And you question people around you why?
When you get to a point where you start to lose your faith
And every emotion inside of you turns to anger and hate
Because you soon come to realize that you're the tragedy of someone's
mistake....

THE LIGHT

As Christians, we know God. It is our faith, it is our belief. But even with knowing God some of us become caught up in 'the world'. I wrote *The Light* in the earlier part of 2007 and when I turned 18, I felt exactly the same way that I was feeling when I wrote that poem. I celebrated my 18th Birthday on September 13th, 2009. It was little over a month into my freshman year of college. I'd started the Broadcasting program and Speech & Debate Season was about to start. I moved out of the dorms and rented a house with two roommates. Everything was a fresh start for me, but for some reason that period was difficult. I was struggling with depression and I wasn't very strong in my faith. I still believed in God but I just didn't want anything to do with God. I felt like God had forsaken me, I don't know why I was feeling that way.

A lot of anger started to build up against my dad. I didn't want anything to do with him. A few weeks after I turned 18, I contacted a lawyer about changing my last name back to Carlson. Carlson was my mom's last name and the last name on my original birth certificate. I thought why should I carry the name of a man who has never done anything for me in my life? The process would be very difficult since all my documents were already in Strachan. So I didn't proceed with the process.

As weeks went by, I sunk deeper and deeper into a depression. It wasn't until my friend Katherine showed concern and suggested that I start counseling. Katherine referred me to a Christian Counseling Agency. I did an intake with one of therapists there. Her name was Jill. She was very nice and I felt a connection with her right away. I requested to have Jill as my therapist and my request was granted. A week after the intake, I went in for my first counseling session. It was a very scary experience. I was expecting traditional counseling but the session was more spiritual and biblical base. At that time I really didn't want to hear anything about God or the bible. I already knew all of the things that she was telling me. I was so tired of people telling me about God and the bible. I wanted to know how to deal with things in the natural not the spiritual. Two sessions in, I stopped counseling.

The following week I went to see Allison who was the counselor at my college to see if she could refer me to an affordable Therapist. She was able to find me an affordable agency. Several days later, I saw a lady named Margaret. I felt so broken. I did another intake and shortly into it I broke down into tears. The session ended shortly after. I continued to see Margaret every other week before taking a short break. A few weeks after the break, I went back in to see Margaret. It was a beautiful sunny day and I was feeling amazing. It was a 360 degree turn around from the way I was feeling when Margaret had last seen me. She was surprise herself. It was a great session. From Margaret's observation that day she said that I could possibly suffer from S.A.D. Seasonal Affective Disorder, which would make sense of the seasonal depression that I experienced. She recommended that on days when the sun was not out, that I would try to find bright lighting. I did just that. I worked through my depression with the help of seeing Margaret and I made it through the end of the semester. Margaret and I concluded our last session in December before I left for the Christmas Break.

The next semester of college, I didn't see Margaret. Speech and Debate and Broadcasting kept me occupied. Between the two, I was very tied up and busy all of the time. I competed in 5 tournaments that semester for Speech and I participated in field projects for Broadcasting. That semester Speech was my main focus. I qualified 2 of my events for Nationals which were held in Athens, Ohio and I spent my time perfecting them. It was in April when my coach and two of my teammates left for Nationals. We stayed at the

Ohio University campus. This was a very exciting time in my life. I was corresponding with my Aunt Janet who was communicating with my dad for me. I spoke to her about asking my dad to help me purchase a car. Aunt Janet said that my dad would. That week in Ohio, I received a phone call from Aunt Janet saying that my dad put some funds on my account towards the purchase of my car. After that phone call I went into my Coach's room where she and my teammates were with tears in my eyes. I couldn't believe it. I couldn't believe that my dad came through for me. It wasn't the fact that he gave me money, it was the fact that he said that he would do something and he did it. In that moment I developed a change in my heart for my dad. I knew that it was time for a change.

CHAPTER FIVE

THERAPY/BACK ON FAITH

"Therefore, if anyone is in Christ, he is a new creation; old things have passed away, behold, all things have become new."
—2 Corinthians 5:17 NKJ

I was born in the Bahamas, a "Christian Nation", into a Christian family and I went to a Christian School. Christianity was all I knew. But even with me growing up as a Christian, it wasn't until I became an adult that I understood the true concept of what being a Christian meant. After Nationals, I left Ohio with a change in my heart. I finished off the semester and I stayed in Norfolk that summer and worked. I received a job at the college, but it wasn't going to start until July. Across the street from where I lived, there was a church. It was on Mother's Day when I decided to visit. I enjoyed the sermon very much and felt very welcomed. I felt like the church was a good fit for me. Little by little I started regaining my faith. That Sunday in the bulletin I saw that the church was in need of a Volunteer Receptionist. Immediately I volunteered. I wanted to help out the church and get know more of the members.

I volunteered once a week for several hours. I mostly answered the phone, send faxes, fold bulletins and did office work. I met a few of the members while volunteering. I also found out that Jill, the therapist that I had seen almost a year before was a member of the church. I continued volunteering until I started my job. That summer I worked until I saved up enough money to purchase a car. It was in mid-July when Donald, the Missions Pastor invited me to attend a College and Young Adult Bible Study that he hosted. I accepted his invitation. I was very nervous, but I enjoyed it. The people there were very friendly and quickly I made new friends. I began to attend church regularly as well as Bible Study. It was great influence over my life.

That following week I went back to the Christian Counseling Agency to see if I could get in to counseling again. I felt like I was ready for it. I wanted to work on my issues, mostly with my dad. I went to the Agency and filled out the paperwork, it took some time to re-process but I waited patiently. I started feeling guilty for the way that I was. I prayed for forgiveness. I wanted to be changed. I wanted to be grounded in my faith and I wanted to be saved, but I didn't know how.

It was a Sunday at church, after the service when I went up to my Pastor Hake's wife.

"Hi Mrs. Hakes, do you know who I can speak with about being saved?" I asked.

"Well, you can speak to my husband," she said with a smile.

We found Pastor Hakes and she and I followed him back to his office. Pastor Hakes talked to me a bit about what it meant to be saved. My perception of things was completely different. He asked me if I was saved before and I told him yes and no. I was a Christian by faith in that I believed in Jesus Christ as the son of God, but I didn't live the Christian life. I professed the ABC (Accept, Believe & Confess) prayer when I was younger but I wanted to be saved as an adult, understanding what it meant to be saved. After we began speaking, Pastor Hakes led us into prayer. He told me the prayer that I needed to pray and that there wasn't a specific prayer, but to just talk to God from my heart. As I began to pour out my heart to God, I broke down into tears. It was a very emotional experience. That day I asked Jesus to come into my heart and I was saved.

After we were done praying, Pastor Hakes gave me a bible. He and his wife both congratulated me and gave me a few scriptures to read. I went back out into the church to mingle for a while. I was talking to a few of the members when Pastor Hakes came by and told them the news. They were all very happy. Out of nowhere, came Jill.

"I don't know if you remember me," she said.

"Yes I remember you, from the Counseling Agency," I replied.

The ladies shared the wonderful news to Jill that I'd just given my life to Christ. She joined in the excitement. I was very happy that Jill had come over. I prayed for a chance to speak with her again. The reason I went back to the Counseling Agency was because I wanted Jill to be my therapist again. I wasn't sure if she would since I'd ended counseling abruptly. Jill left to speak with another member in the church while I continued to speak with the two ladies. I noticed that Jill was leaving so I excused myself to speak with her before she left.

"Hey Jill, it was ironic that you came over because I went to the Counseling Agency last week to see if I can get back into counseling," I said.

"That's good, I'm happy for you," she said with a smile.

"Thanks, I wanted to know if you could be my therapist because I really liked you as a therapist," I said to her.

"Thanks, well of course, I'll look forward to seeing you," Jill smiled.

I smiled as Jill left. I was happy that she was okay with being my therapist again.

The next week I got a call from the agency saying that I could set up an appointment. That very week, almost a year later, I went back in and met with Jill. There were so many things to discuss. We first talked about what went wrong the first time and what we could do differently. I told her that I wanted less biblical-base counseling and more traditional counseling. She respected and supported my decision. I started seeing Jill once a week. Immediately we began working on the issues with my dad. I did most of the talking. Talking about my dad brought so many feelings. Feelings of hurt, abandonment, feeling unloved, unwanted just so many different emotions. But it was what I needed to go through in order to heal.

After a few sessions, Jill gave me an assignment. The assignment was to write a letter to my dad and to read it to him. I avoided writing the letter, but I knew that it was something that I had to do. The day before my next counseling session Jill, I emotionally detached myself and wrote the letter to my dad. The next day I went to counseling.

"Are you ready?" asked Jill.

"I guess," I replied.

"I want you to pretend that your dad is sitting in that chair and I want you to read the letter to him," said Jill.

I took a deep breath and read the letter to my dad and broke down into tears. The feeling was overwhelming. But I knew that it was what I had to do, to let those emotions out. After reading through two difficult pages I was done. I did it! For the first time in my life I verbally expressed my feelings towards my dad. I felt relieved. For the first month and a half I worked through the issues with my dad. As I began healing, Jill and I started to talk about forgiveness.

"Do you think that you're at a place where you can forgive your dad?" Jill would ask me.

"I don't know, I'll have to talk to him," would be my response.

It was hard to think about forgiving him, for all the years of neglect. I wanted to talk to him. I wanted to know, what were his reasons for abandoning me?

"Well why don't you call him?" Jill suggested.

I thought about it for some time and eventually I decided

to call. I called Aunt Janet and asked her if she could connect me to my dad. That night for the first time in over two years I talked to my dad. I heard the joy in his voice when we spoke. We didn't speak very long due to the bad connection between the phones. But my dad told me that he would call me the next day after 3. I waited the next day for my dad to call and he didn't. I saw Jill that evening and told her that I spoke with my dad.

"How did it go?" she asked.

"It was so-so and it was nice hearing from him but we didn't really get to talk," I said with disappointment.

"He also said he was going to call me today but he didn't."

I was upset about it. Once again another broken promise from my dad, I thought he'd changed. This made the thought about forgiving him even harder. Jill suggested that I call him again but I didn't want to waste my time.

Two months had gone by and it was now the earlier part of October. I was still working on my issues with my dad. It was a conversation that I had with my mom that I developed a change of heart. My mom ran into my Aunt Angie, my dad's older sister who told my mom that my dad was a "sick man". I didn't know what she meant by sick but it made me sad. I knew that my dad developed seizures due to him being attacked and I knew that he was an alcoholic. I reflected on that for some time and it made me think. What is being angry at my dad doing for me? It's not affecting him because he doesn't even know. It was only affecting me. I went in and saw Jill that day and told her about the conversation with my mom. I broke down into tears. I felt so bad. I told Jill that the past didn't matter anymore and that I forgave my dad. I wanted to work things out between us. Jill was very pleased by this. After that I thought about my dad a lot. I began making plans to visit my dad for the

Christmas break.

During this time, I found out from Aunt Janet that Grammy Mabel was battling cancer. That week I went out and bought her a 'Get Well Soon' Card and I bought my dad a 'Thank You' Card for helping me with school supplies that August. I decided not to mail the cards because I wanted to send a photo of myself to both my grandmother and my dad because I knew that they didn't have any recent photos of me. Things were going well and then tragedy struck. My step-cousin Cameron was electrocuted. That weekend while he fought for his life in the ICU. I was competing at a Speech Tournament in Omaha. I didn't talk to my family because they were all at the hospital but I found out through Facebook that he died. It was so sad. A few weeks later my Instructor Mrs. Anderson lost her dad and Speech Coach Joanne was dealing with her dad's terminal cancer. I felt like I was seeing so much of death. It made me miss my dad. I thought to myself what if I was to lose him? I had to talk to him. I had to write to him so that week I wrote him this letter.

Letter #1   November 2010

Dear Daddy,

I hope everything is well with you. I wanted to send you a thank you card for coming through for me once again. I greatly appreciate it. I thought it would be cool to write you because I haven't spoken to you or seen you in years. I don't know, I feel kind of down today and I thought about you. Daddy people around me are dying and it really makes you think how precious life is. I lost my step-cousin two weeks ago; he was Alex's friend also. Alex was actually one of the paul bearers and my mom got a chance to speak with him. He has a beautiful son; I've seen his pictures on Facebook. I think you should get a Facebook :), so you can keep up to date with us. I am happy to say that I have Sasha, Alex, Estelle and Anthony on my Facebook. Daddy I wish we were a lot closer, but it seems like everyone is just caught up in their own lives. I want so badly to know my family and to have a strong relationship with everyone, but daddy I'm just tired of reaching out. It really makes me sad the way things are. It seems that death is the only thing that brings a family together and it shouldn't have to be that way.

But in all honesty I really want to feel like I belong. I use to think when I was younger that maybe if I was famous then maybe I could have my family because I do really want those relationships, even with you. Daddy you know I was at a place where I was so bitter and angry at you and I spent two months in Counseling just talking about you because I always felt unloved and unwanted and I became such an angry person, but two months later I'm at a place where I have peace. I had to find it in myself to forgive and let go. I'm a born again Christian and I think the hardest struggle I faced was forgiveness. I knew I reached to that place when I told my therapist that I wouldn't have any angry words for you if I spoke to you again and I don't. I just pray to God to keep you safe and well.

I don't know how you're doing but I really hope all is well with you. I don't know why but in a sense I feel like I'm losing you and I don't want to lose you, which is weird because I never even had you. I miss you daddy, I miss having a dad and I feel sad because I think that it's going to be something that I never have. I guess I'm feeling this way because my Speech Coach leaves for Arizona to visit with her dad because he's in his last stages of Cancer. I don't want that to be me. You know daddy, I'm a very independent person with a lot of stubbornness and pride and I always think that I don't need help from people. That I don't need people in general because they're always going to let you down. But you know I realize that sometimes we just think that we have the answers to everything and that we're okay and there's nothing wrong with us. I was that same way and it really gets you in a dark place, but you know once you have people there to help you get through its amazing.

You know this summer I decided to go see a therapist because I realized that I was so angry, hurt and bitter about everything in my life and it was one of the best decisions I made in life. I am a new and different person because of it and trust me I have A LOT of pride. My mom doesn't even know. But I realize that if you need help then you should get it. People have this stigma that people who see a therapist are crazy. It's like if you had a pain in your body you would see a doctor. Emotional and psychological pains are that way, people hurt so they need to see someone to make those feelings go away. I guess what I'm saying is take care of yourself and just keep yourself well. If you need help physically or psychologically don't be afraid to get it. Life is precious and it's short so just live it to the best of you. I really do love you daddy. Take care, be safe and know that you are always in my thoughts and prayers.

Love Always,

Your Baby girl Shanea

I never got the chance to send my letter and he never got to read it and I struggled with the regret of not sending it for a very long time.

CHAPTER SIX
FAMILY BUSINESS PART II

Today I shed a tear for you,
Welcome to the world.
I may never get to hold you, or even know you
But nephew, I love you.
I hope and pray that your dad be the best dad that he can be
And be everything to you that our father never was.
You are born into a family who loves you and they always will.
Auntie's baby, my nephew…
Who's name yet I do not know…
I love you so much and I will be watching you as you grow.

TO MY NEPHEW 5/19/10

Rewinding back to May of that year, I wrote this poem for my nephew when he was born. I was friends with my brother Alex on Facebook for several months but we never spoke to each other. I found out through his Facebook that he was expecting his first son. I felt so excited about being an aunt and knowing that I had a nephew on the way. I loved him so much already, despite the fact that there would be a chance that I would never know him. Several months later my oldest brother Anthony added me on Facebook and I found that I had another nephew. I was now connected to all of my siblings. My big brother Anthony and I talked a lot. He wanted to meet when I came home that Christmas. It was cool because Anthony knew my best friends Alannah, Andrew and Ethan.

Time went by quickly and in no time it was December. After two long days of travelling and a five hour boat ride, I returned home after 11 months. It felt good to be back at home. When I arrived home the first thing that I did was call my dad. I couldn't wait to talk to him. I made plans to visit him sometime during my trip, but my plans weren't finalized. I called my dad on the 22nd of December. He didn't sound very well and we didn't talk very long. He told me that he had been at home sick for the past three weeks and that he would call me once he was feeling better. Immediately after speaking with my dad, I called Aunt Janet. She told me that he wasn't doing well, he had lost a large amount of weight and he was having difficulty breathing. It sounded serious so I asked her if I should come to Nassau. She insisted that I should. I told Aunt Janet that I would sleep on it and give her a call the next day.

I didn't really think too much about it because my dad told me that he would be alright. The next day I called Aunt Janet to find out if my dad was feeling any better and she told me that she had just came from by my Aunt Tangie's house where my dad was staying. She told me that my dad still wasn't doing well and he didn't want to go and see a doctor.

"Shanea, talk to your daddy and see if you could talk some sense into him," said my Aunt Janet as she connected me to my dad.

He answered the phone.

"Hi, daddy, my mind came across you today and I thought I would call to see how you doing," I said.

"I'm okay, baby, man Shanea daddy really ain't feeling well but as soon as I feel better I'll call you," he said.

"What's wrong though?" I asked.

"Must be a cold or something," he said breathing faintly on the line.

"You know when you're feeling sick you should really go to the doctor because these days you just don't know," I said.

"I gen go to the doctor tomorrow," he replied with agitation.

There was a brief silence.

"Well, I want you to know that I'm praying for you," I said breaking the silence.

"Thank you," he responded.

"I love you," were the words that came out of my mouth.

"Love you too, baby," he replied.

That was the end of our conversation. My dad did keep his word and went to the doctor the next day. I called Grammy Mabel and she told me that the doctors said that he didn't have any minerals in his body and they gave him vitamins to build up his immune system. A day later I spoke to my big brother Anthony and we made plans to meet each other. It was Christmas Eve, when Anthony and I first met. It was a very happy moment for me. We talked for quite some time and made plans to hang out before I went back to school.

It was a joyous time being home for Christmas. I celebrated Christmas Eve in church with my mom and my little sister Sade. Christmas day came and it was wonderful. There were lots of gifts under the tree and later that day my family got together for Christmas Dinner. It was indeed the most wonderful time of the year. Two days after Christmas on the 27th of December around 12 in the morning, I received a call from Aunt Janet. She called me to let me know that my dad was admitted into the hospital because he was having difficulty breathing again. Aunt Janet had faith that he was going to be okay. We talked for almost an hour, before hanging up the phone.

Shortly after 6 that morning, the phone rang. My best friend Alannah, who spent the night, brought the cordless phone into mom's room. She said that it was my aunt. Immediately I knew that something wasn't right. I'd just spoken to Aunt Janet a few hours before. My mom took the phone and the sound in her voice confirmed that something was wrong.

"Oh Lord, I'll tell Shanea," I heard my mom say.

That very instant I got up.

"My daddy died didn't he?" I asked my mom.

She hung up the phone and said yes. I couldn't believe it. I didn't want to believe it. I had just spoken to my dad a few days before. I called Aunt Janet back to find out if it was true. She answered the phone in tears. That morning I called both of my brothers but they didn't answer. I went on Facebook later that day to see if they were online, but they weren't.

I didn't know how to feel. My mom had just told me that my dad died. I knew that I was sad and I felt sad about it but I really didn't have any emotions. A part of it just didn't feel real. I kept myself together for the sake of my mom and my little sister. I didn't want them to see that I was affected by it. They were very supportive and so was Alannah. That day, I posted a R.I.P tribute to my dad on my Facebook page that said,

> I wish someone could shake me and wake me up from this bad dream and I wish I had gotten on that plane to come and see you...... now it's too late..... I'm here just missing you like crazy..... I love you daddy.........7/25/61 - 12/27/10.

I attached the Whitney Houston song, *Where Does Broken Hearts Go*. I mean where did they go? That song explained exactly how I felt. I really didn't know where to take my broken heart. I received a lot of condolences from friends on Facebook and I appreciated the support. That day I just laid in bed, I didn't know what else to do. Later in the afternoon, I went outside and called Grammy Mabel to check in on how things were in Nassau.

"So you heard your daddy dead aye?" she asked.

"Yes ma'am, what happened though?" I asked.

"Shanea, Eddie had so many things wrong with him..." replied Grammy Mabel.

She went on to tell me that my dad had a mass which the doctors suspected to be cancer, fluid in his lungs and also suffered from a seizure. When I heard everything that went wrong with my dad I broke down into tears. I cried at the fact that he suffered what sounded to be a painful death. He didn't deserve it, nobody deserved it. I hung up the phone from Grammy Mabel. I sat outside until I was able to regain myself.

An hour or so later I received a call from Estelle. She was at Aunt Tangie's and was calling to find out how I was doing. We didn't speak very long but she asked me if I was okay. I told her yes. I was happy to hear from Estelle, but I really didn't feel like talking to anyone. I told Estelle that I would talk to her later.

"Okay… love you," she said.

"Love you too," I responded.

I hung up the phone. That was a very special moment for me because that was the first time that I had ever heard "Love you" from my big sister. I slept for the rest afternoon. Later Aunt Angie came by the house to visit me. I gave her a big hug. I was so happy to see her. She stayed for a while before leaving.

Things went back to normal that week. My mom went back to work and Sade and I stayed at home. The week after my dad's death, all I did was sleep. I slept for hours and hours at a time, day and night. I didn't want to feel the reality of it. I spoke with Aunt Janet on a weekly basis as my family in Nassau made preparations for my dad's funeral. I wanted to be involved and I wanted to be a part of what was going on. All of my life I felt like an outside child. So disconnected from dad's side of the family. Now more than ever I wanted to be connected with them. Connected to people who knew how I felt and who shared the same pain that I did. The week before my dad's funeral, I made the decision to go to Nassau to spend time with the family that I never knew.

CHAPTER SEVEN

THE OTHER HALF OF ME: MY REALITY

"The hardest part about reality was the realness that everything that passed is my life."
—Shanea A. Strachan

On Monday January 10th, which was also the first day of classes of my spring semester of college, I boarded an airplane to Nassau with my Aunt Angie and my three cousins. There was a deep pain in my stomach. We made a safe landing into Nassau. Aunt Angie's friend picked us up and dropped us off by Aunt Tangie's house. We were greeted with hugs by Grammy Mabel. It felt strange being in the house where my dad stayed. I sat in Grammy Mabel's room as they began talking about my dad. As they started to talk about him I grew emotional. I stayed by Aunt Tangie's house until Aunt Janet came to pick me and my cousins up. We were staying by Aunt Janet for the week.

The first two days in Nassau was spent making funeral preparations. Talking back and forth with the funeral home and making sure that everything was in order for the viewing and for the funeral service. I spent my days mostly out and about with my aunts. My brother Alex came over on the third day. I was at Aunt Tangie's when we first met. That night Estelle came by, it was nice to finally see her. Alex seemed cool. He, my cousins and I all stayed by Aunt Janet that night. I didn't have much to say. I didn't know what to say. As time went by it became easier and we all began to talk and get along. It was now Thursday. My big brother Anthony was coming over with my nephew and I was excited to finally meet him. Sasha was the only one who wasn't able to attend the funeral. Alannah was coming over the next day and I was happy to have her support. I met a lot of my family for the first time while I was in Nassau. I was sad that it took the death of my dad to meet them, but all in all I was happy that I was able to meet them. That Thursday I stayed at Aunt Tangie's house while my Aunt Sidra and my brother Alex went out. They came back a few hours later with one of my dad's friend. The lady looked very familiar.

"Alex, who is that?" I asked.

"Daddy's sugar," he replied.

When they said her name, it came back to me. It was Diane. My dad's girlfriend who I had met many years before. She and my dad were still together at the time of his death. When she got into the room with Grammy Mabel, the two of them started to cry. Here we go, I thought to myself. After they calmed down I went into the room to introduce myself to Diane. She gave me a hug and told me how much I had grown. Later that day I went by my grand-aunt Evelyn's Dress Shop with Aunt Angie to steam press our dresses for the funeral. We stayed there until night. That night I went back to Aunt Janet's house with my cousins and Alex. My big brother Anthony missed his flight and wasn't coming until the morning.

The next morning, I woke up with yet another pain in my stomach. It was the day of the viewing of the body of my dad. When I was done getting dressed, Anthony and my nephew was there. I was so happy to see them, especially my nephew. Shortly after, we all loaded up in Aunt Janet's car and headed over to the funeral home. When we arrived Grammy Mabel, Aunt Angie and my grandaunt Evelyn along with a few other family members and Diane was seated in the lobby. Grammy Mabel and Aunt Angie were already crying. I felt a deep pain in my stomach as the man from the funeral home came out and took my Grammy's hand. He leaded her to the back room. She disappeared around the corner and the next thing I heard was screaming. Aunt Angie went in next with my two cousins and then Diane followed. More screams was heard. My stomach really began to hurt. My brother Alex went in and I stood out front for a brief minute with Anthony. I took a deep breath and slowly walked towards the room. As I walked closer and closer the sounds of crying got louder. I said to myself,

"I'm not going to cry, I'm not going to cry, I'm not going

to cry…" I repeated.

I walked up to my dad's casket and looked at him.

"Daddy…" I cried out.

Immediately I dropped to the floor in tears. I couldn't contain myself, the emotions just came. I looked at my dad for a good minute just crying. Him just lying there, he looked so different. Not like the dad that I had known. Alex stood there next to me looking at our dad with tears falling down his face.

I backed up out of the room and went to where Anthony was with my nephew. I held my nephew for a while so that Anthony could go in and see our dad. He came out shortly after. I went back in the room thinking that I would be stronger but I broke down into tears again. I walked out of the room and cried to myself in the hallway. Just crying and wanting so badly to be comforted and consoled by someone. My family didn't seem like the affectionate type so I stood there for a good while just crying. In that moment, I wanted my mom so badly. It was the most horrible feeling that I had ever felt. It was a heaven sent when Diane came over and comforted me. She held me and cried along with me as I cried in her arms.

"I love your daddy," she said.

I believed that she did because of what she had just done for me. After sometime I went back into the room and stood next to Alex.

"You okay?" I asked.

He didn't respond. We just stood there and stared at our dad as 'What a Wonderful World' by Louis Armstrong played on repeat. It didn't seem like a wonderful world that day. Later that night Alannah came over to Aunt Tangie's house and took me out. After a sad day, I was happy to be out with my best friend. She introduced me to her friends Julian and Hakeem who were our dates for the night. They were very polite. They took us to Arawak Cay for some Conch Salad. I was happy to be with my best friend and I was happy that she was in Nassau for my dad's funeral. I enjoyed the night out. I returned to Aunt Janet's around 11 pm that night and went straight to bed.

The next morning everyone got up early for the funeral. The pain in my stomach was back. My brothers, cousins and Aunt Janet all got ready and headed over to Aunt Tangie's house. Most of my family was there. I was happy when I arrived and Grammy Mabel told me that my mom was in Aunt Tangie's room. I gave my mom a big hug when I saw her. We talked for a while until it was time to leave. I loaded up into the limousine with my mom, my two cousins, my brother Alex and my sister Estelle and we made our way to the church. When we arrived my mom went inside to find a seat while the coordinator from the funeral home lined up the family in the order we were to proceed in and inside we proceeded. When I got into the church, I was happy to see Alannah who was seated next to my mom. I made my way down to the seats in the front of the church that were re-served for us. I sat between my Aunt Tangie and my cousin. I watched as people walked to the front of the church to view my dad's body. Grammy Mabel went up to say her final goodbye to my dad, while my big brother Anthony supported her. She couldn't contain her tears. The coordina-tor from the funeral home made the announcement that the casket was going to be closed soon. I took a deep breath and walked over to say my last goodbye to my dad. I put my hand on his chest and then on his head.

"Good-bye, daddy, I love you," I whispered.

Everyone said their last goodbyes and sat back down as

the coordinator slowly closed the casket. As he slowly closed the casket, Aunt Janet came up to have her last moments with my dad. The two of them were the closest and she watched in tears until the very end as the casket closed and my dad's body was no longer seen. Aunt Janet broke down into tears. She was so strong through everything and kept it all together with dealing with the funeral plans. After the casket was closed, the funeral service started.

My dad's funeral was the first funeral that I attended in many years. I sat there as the service went on. About mid-way into the service I did a tribute for my dad. The funeral service continued as tribute after tribute went on and friends of my dad came up to speak. I listened attentively as some of my dad's closest friends shared heartfelt memories of him. What touched me was a memory shared by one of my dad's classmates. My dad celebrated his Class Reunion in October of that year and she talked about how she remembered my dad on the night of the reunion. She spoke to him that night and she told the church about how much he talked about his children, especially his daughters and how he was so proud of us. Even when she changed the topic he would go back to talking about his children. That brought me so much comfort in hearing that. The lady then asked us to identify ourselves,

"Where are the children?" she asked.

We all raised our hands.

"I want you'll to know that your father loved you all very much," she concluded.

The service concluded with a prayer and a recessional hymn. We proceeded out and loaded back into the limousines and made our way to the burial site.

It was long drive to the graveyard. The car was filled with

silence. Estelle turned on the radio breaking the silence. *Moment for Life* by Nicki Minaj played as I bopped my head to the song and recited the words softly. In that moment, I did want that moment for life. The moment of being around all of my family. Coincidently when that song ended we are at the graveyard. Again came the stomach pain as we pulled into the graveyard and drove up to my dad's burial site. We got out and sat in the seats that were prepared for us. Aunt Angie sat next to Grammy Mabel, which left me sitting in the second row by myself. I remember sitting in the back of my brothers and Estelle feeling like how I felt my entire life by my dad's family, like the outside child. In that moment I wished that Sasha was there. It was Estelle who broke that feeling when she called me over to sit closer by them. My brother Alex got a white rose from dad's casket for each of us and the burial service proceeded shortly after. I tried my hardest to remain strong through the service, but it was when they began lowering my dad into the grave was when I lost it. My mom came over and consoled me. I calmed down after a while. The Minister made the final remarks. It was then that my sister Estelle reached back and held my hand. In that moment even though I wasn't seated with my siblings I felt connected to them. After the Minister was with the closing remarks, the service ended and my dad was buried. I walked over to Alannah who was waiting for me with open arms. She walked me back to the limousine. I was happy to have her and my mom there. I was thankful that Alannah made the sacrifice to travel all the way to Nassau to support me.

After the burial service, everyone went over to Aunt Tangie's house where the family got together. My grandaunts and other family members prepared food while everyone socialized and reminisced about past times and memories of my dad. It was great to see so many family members. Everyone seemed very happy. I was happy. This was the moment that I wanted for life. I met family members whom I had never even knew of. I had aunts, uncles and lots of cousins. My family was very big. I spent a lot of time with my nephew, who was just about 18 months and I took lots photos that day. Grammy Mabel seemed happy to have her children, her grandchildren and even her great-grand child around. We stayed at Aunt Tangie's house until night. That night my aunts took my brothers, my sister, my cousins and I out to a little pub. We ate conch fritters and played pool. It was a wonderful night. Anthony and I talked a lot that night. He reminded me so much of myself, kind, humble and sweet. We talked about so many different things and played pool against each other. He of course beat me in two games of pool [laughs]. That night while I played pool with my siblings the song *No Woman No Cry* by Bob Marley blasted through the Jukebox. It was the words "Everything is going to be alright" that sung repetitively that stood out to me. In my heart I felt like my dad saying that to me through the song.

At the end of the night I went back to Aunt Janet's house where I spent my last night in Nassau. I went to bed shortly after I got in. The next morning at 6 am, my mom arrived to pick me up. I said goodbye to Aunt Janet and then left with my mom to the airport. We took the 7 am flight to Grand Bahama and about 35 minutes later we were back home. I was happy to be home again and I spent the day at home until it was time for me to embark on another journey and begin living my life after my dad's death.

CHAPTER EIGHT
GRIEVING & FAITH

Constantly inconsistent
The way it has been from the beginning
The constancy of people being inconsistent in my life
Here today, gone tomorrow....
Maybe a few weeks or months, I'll see you or hear from you
again.
Inconsistent from the beginning
Like a farmer you planted your seed
Inconsistency from lack of constancy
A relationship that should have blossomed into a flower is now
just a weed.
Constantly like my memory that plays back the constant in-
consistency of others,
Constantly hurt
Constantly lied too
But still...
Foolishly always forgiving and opening myself up to constant
"inconsistencies".

CONSTANTLY INCONSISTENT

The grieving process for me was very difficult. Grief is never easy. The poem *Constantly Inconsistent* reminded me a lot of my grieving process. I always felt that a lot of people were inconsistent in my life and I wrote *Constantly Inconsistent* about a situation that I experienced. I tied my dad into the poem because our relationship was the most inconsistent. But it was while grieving his death was when I felt inconsistencies the most. There were people that showed concern in the beginning when I lost my dad and that was it. There were people that I thought would show concern and didn't. What hurt me about that, were that they were people whom I had personally talk to one on one about my dad and our relationships. It really bothered me.

I think that was one of the hardest parts about grieving for me because I felt like a lot of people didn't care. I spoke to Jill about those feelings and she suggested that I should try reaching out to those people. I apposed that. I was always the initiator when it came to reaching out. I was always the one trying to make relationships work. Jill challenged me to change my thinking about it. But I felt like I was grieving alone. I felt like I needed to be connected to people who understood what I was going through and those people were my siblings and my dad's family. I wanted to talk to them, not necessarily about my dad but just to talk to them.

On several occasions I tried reaching out to my sister Sasha but she would always shoot me down. I would try talking to her and she would all of the sudden go offline or I would send her messages that she never responded too. I never understood why she was that way towards me. I had never done anything to her. I always felt like Sasha was punishing me for what my dad did or didn't do and that wasn't fair. Estelle was hardly ever online so I couldn't really talk to her and it was just different with my brothers.

I went through these feelings for the first month of griev-

ing my dad's death. On the one month anniversary of my
dad's death, I wrote a note on my Facebook and tagged my
family members on my dad's side in it. It read,

> I remember saying to a friend yesterday that today
> was going to be a really LONG day. The reason be-
> ing is because today makes 1 month since my dad
> died. Yesterday I woke up with the thought on my
> mind, that a month ago today was my dad's last day
> on earth. So many thoughts raced through my head
> and a feeling of sadness took over me. It felt as if
> it was December all over again and that I was just
> waiting for something that I knew was going to hap-
> pen. Last night I found myself parked in my car for
> about an hour just screaming at the top of my lungs
> and crying uncontrollably. Eventually I ended up at
> a friend's house and then I ended up home. I woke
> up at 6 am this morning, like I did a month ago,
> expecting the news that I already had.

> I guess the reason why I am writing this is because
> like the title says, "life doesn't just go on..." I come
> from a culture where it seems like bad things can
> happen to people; you go through it, put a smile on
> your face and live the rest of your life like nothing
> ever happened. Six months ago I made the decision
> to start seeing a Therapist. A decision that not even
> my mom knew about. Why? Because the cultural
> norm that I've grew up in is that only "crazy" people
> go through therapy. I've always looked at it this way,
> if I have chest pains, I'm going to go to a doctor to
> help get rid of that pain. So if I'm hurting emotion-
> ally, why shouldn't I go to someone who can help
> me get rid of that hurt? It's just a different kind of
> pain. Therapy has brought me along way and has
> helped me a lot with coming to a place of peace and

forgiveness with my dad before he passed and I am so thankful for that. I have never before in my life loss someone close to me and I won't lie it is hard. But I am learning to take things one day at a time. Grief is not an overnight process, and you just don't feel better the next day.

I guess I want to end this by saying to all of you who are going through what I'm going through or went through this is to don't ever be afraid to seek help and don't ever be afraid to tell people how you really feel. I mean it's alright to tell people that, "I'm going through a really hard time right now", or "I could really use a hug". We are human beings not robots and we feel. Everybody wants someone to care. After seeing my therapist and shedding some tears, today doesn't feel like such a long day anymore. I don't know what tomorrow will bring, but today I can say that I am doing just fine.

I wanted people to see that I was human. I wanted people to know how I felt and what I was going through. I got a great deal of responses from quite a few people but the response that surprised me the most was the response from my sister Sasha.

"Life has a funny way of making you appreciate it...I understand completely where you coming from...I'm not the best example of a sister but I'm working on it...don't want to come half stepping...just know that when I have completely mastered sibling love it's going to be extraordinary... just hope I won't be too late....." was her reply.

"Thanks sis, this means a lot coming from you. I know that you understand where I'm coming from and I understand where you are coming from also. But know that it will never be too late; my heart will always be open for my siblings. Especially my sisters." I replied.

I was happy that Sasha read the note, more so that she took the time to respond. We never talked after that but this showed me that to some extent Sasha cared. I was excited to share this news with Jill. She was very happy for me. At the end of our session, we prayed for more breakthroughs with the relationship with my siblings. They came from time to time. I felt like going through the grieving process, I needed them. I just wanted to feel connected in a way to people who understood and could relate to what I was going through.

Grief came in a variety of stages. There were days when life felt unreal, days when I felt normal and other days when I felt extremely sad. I couldn't grasp this concept of death and what it meant to lose someone. My dad stayed on my mind daily. I constantly thought about him. Another phase of grief that I experienced was guilt. A lot of guilt consumed me and I spent a lot of time crying about it. I loved my dad but I felt guilty over the things that I had said about him over the years. Guilty by the way I talked about him. Jill told me that this was normal. To help me through the grieving process, I wrote my dad letters.

In the midst of all of the pain and hurt of grieving I found time to talk to God. Mostly during times when I was down. I would always end up in tears, crying out to Him and would somehow after praying feel comforted. It was a feeling of arms being wrapped around me, like I was being hugged by angels. I was open and honest to God about how I felt. I was confused and angry about everything that happened. About going through counseling to work on the issues with my dad and finally reaching a place where I was ready to make things work and him being taken away. God had a lot of explaining to do. I continued praying and I would always somehow be directed to a scripture in the bible that spoke to me about what I talked to God about.

I took it as God's way of communicating with me. After a while, I accepted everything. I knew that there was a reason that everything happened the way it did. When I found the letter that I wrote to my dad a month before his death it was then that I realized what the purpose of it was. I went through everything so that I could be prepared to do God's work. I was now a testimony and my job was to share my story and help others find strength in forgiveness.

CHAPTER NINE

IT DOESN'T JUST GO ON...

It's been almost seven months since you left me
And these tears still flow from my eyes
Laying here with thoughts running through my mind
Wishing that you could have been here
For a much longer time
Hoping that things would change and we'd all be fine
But this is all in my head and can never be
Because Daddy you flew away from me
Your energy disbursed into a Universe unknown
But I know you're still here and I'm never alone
Because in my Heart you'll forever live on
I picture you as my Guardian Angel
Watching over me.

I knew that you loved me
Even though we were far apart
I forgave your mistakes
Because you were my dad.
You are one of the reasons for my existence
Without you I would have never been formed
And for that mere fact I try to stay strong

I love you Daddy I truly do Forever and Always
With Love,
From your Daughter to You...... ..

Happy Birthday Daddy by Estelle

On July 25th, 2011 was what would have been my dad's 50th birthday. I spent the day on a Greyhound bus, making my way back to Norfolk, Nebraska. I remember at a stop Tennessee looking out of the window at a father who was hugging and kissing his children goodbye. I admired that. I saw several few fathers with their children on some of the stops that we made. I was happy for those children because their dads were present in their lives. I cried that day as I spoke to my dad and wished him Happy Birthday. Towards the end of the night, the bus made a stop at a food place. I was finally able to check my Facebook and I noticed that Estelle wrote a poem for our dad. When I read it, I knew that I wanted to conclude my story with Estelle's poem.

As children no matter how much we say that we hate our parents, deep down inside we still love them. My dad was far from perfect. He made many mistakes, he broke many promises and he disappointed me in many ways. As much as I loved my dad, I hated him because of all of those things. Hate is like a disease that can spread and harm us in so many ways. I came to the realization that in hating my dad, I was only harming myself. I knew that I had to let go of that hate because my dad wasn't the one hurting from it, I was. I did the work and I started to take care of myself and I released that hate. Today I am doing just okay. I am living my life and I'm sharing my story. I've been through a lot and I've fell many times but I got right back up. My hope of sharing my story is to let you know that the power is in you to change any situation. Remember that you are the most important person, so always take care of yourself first. I also want to say never lose faith because God never leaves us. I like to think of the song 'Footprints in the Sand'. When we look back in our lives at the hard times and notice that there's only one set of footprints in the sand it was during those times that God is carrying us.

I want to touch briefly once more on grief. Grief is probably one of the hardest things that a person will ever deal with. When people grieve know that they need you. They want you to reach out. Most of the time people only show concern for the first few weeks and they assume that it would be best to leave things alone or to not bring things up. I can't speak for everyone, but I know that I wanted people's continued support. Someone once told me that time heals all wounds. But to people who are grieving sometimes the pain gets harder as time goes by. So in the days, weeks, months or even years later always remember the grieving hearts. Writing this book has been a two year journey and I am happy that this journey has finally come to an end. Thank you for reading my story.

"Life Doesn't JUST Go On…"

Artwork on previous page by Shanique Ariel Kemp

Shanea Strachan is a Media Artist, who was born and raised in Freeport, Bahamas. In her spare time, she enjoys writing, photography, filmmaking and cooking. She is currently a Media Arts major at New Mexico Highlands University and resides in Las Vegas, New Mexico.

Life Doesn't Just Go On... is her first published book.

Readers may contact Shanea through her website:
www.shaneastrachan.com
Or at the following mailing address:
P.O.Box 9064
Las Vegas, NM 87701